Getting started with

KEYBOARD
MUSICIANSHIP

beginner to grade 3

by Nicholas Keyworth

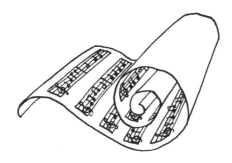

TRINITY · FABER

Faber Music 3 Queen Square London WC1N 3AU

in association with

Trinity College *London* 89 Albert Embankment London SE1 7TP

Foreword

This book introduces keyboard musicianship in an enjoyable and approachable way. It is written to help teachers incorporate elements of transposition and keyboard harmony into music lessons.

The stimulating ideas are designed to be introduced in the lesson and then worked on at home by the pupil as part of their practice time.

By the end of the book pupils will have developed many basic keyboard skills which will help them learn pieces more quickly, sight read more effectively, make a start with improvisation and be capable and confident of opting for keyboard musicianship in their exams. The skills learnt will also be transferable and useful to other instruments.

Fingering has been suggested in some of the exercises.

Answers for all the numbered questions in the book are available on the *Getting started* website: www.fabermusic.com/gettingstarted

© 2004 by Faber Music Ltd and Trinity College *London*
First published in 2004 by Faber Music Ltd
in association with Trinity College *London*
3 Queen Square London WC1N 3AU
Cover illustration by Jan McCafferty
Music processed by Stave Origination
Printed in England by Caligraving Ltd

ISBN 0–571–52136–1

To buy Faber Music or Trinity publications or to find out about the full range of titles available please contact your local music retailer or Faber Music sales enquiries:

Faber Music Ltd, Burnt Mill, Elizabeth Way, Harlow CM20 2HX
Tel: +44 (0)1279 82 89 82   Fax: +44 (0)1279 82 89 83
sales@fabermusic.com   fabermusic.com   trinitycollege.co.uk

Getting started

Look at this shape and imagine how it would sound played as a melody:

Starting on middle C, play the shape.
Did it sound how you imagined it would? _____

Choose a new note to start on: _____ and play the shape again.
Did the melody sound the same?

_____

Can you add your own dynamics as well when you play this?

Here is the shape above shown as notes. By showing it on a stave we can be more accurate about which notes to play. Can you see the shape you have been playing in these notes?

Drawing musical lines

Draw each of these melodies as a line, then play each shape starting on the notes given under the boxes.

[ ] Play the shape starting on another **C** on the keyboard.
[ ] Play the shape starting on **G**.

[ ] Play the shape starting on **E.**
[ ] Play the shape starting on **C.**

Did you have to play any black notes to make the melodies sound right?

Steps and jumps

So far, we've looked at music that moves mainly by step so it's easy to see the shape as a line. Look at this melody:

① Circle any pairs of notes that move by a jump in the melody above.
   Draw the melody; remembering to show the jumps between notes:

Now play it
❑ starting on **G**.
❑ starting on **C** in the left hand.
Do you recognise the melody?

Have a go at draw
your own tunes in Gett
started with compositi

Your own pieces

Think about the first two bars of two pieces you are learning, without looking at the music. Then fill in and complete the following on each piece:

Piece title: _____

Draw the shape of the first two bars here:

❑ First note: _____
❑ Play it starting one note higher.
❑ Play it starting one note lower.

Piece title: _____

Draw the shape of the first two bars here:

❑ First note: _____
❑ Play it starting one note higher.
❑ Play it starting one note lower.

Try to remember
if the notes move
by step or jump.

Completing melodies

Here is one bar of a melody starting on A. Play this then complete the second bar using only the notes A B C D E. When you're happy with how it sounds then write it down:

Think about dynamics when you play this: is it better loud or soft?

Now play the same melody starting on **D**. When you're happy with how it sounds, write it down:

Here is the beginning of another melody, this time starting on D. Complete the final bar, ending on D, using only the notes D, F♯ and A.

Remember to play it first then write it down when you're happy with it.

This time play the melody:
- ❏ Starting on **E**.
- ❏ Starting on a **black note**.

To make melodies sound exactly the same wherever we play them on the keyboard, we need to know more about keys and patterns of tones and semitones.

Shapes everywhere…

Get a friend or a teacher to play the opening of one of their pieces. Draw it as a shape then try playing it yourself. Don't worry if it doesn't sound the same! Talk about any differences you can hear.

Think about a school song, nursery rhyme or the opening music of your favourite TV programme. Can you hear the shape of the melody? Can you draw or play any of it?

Tones and semitones

To understand tones and semitones it's easiest to look at the piano keyboard. All the notes are laid out in order; the black notes are the sharp and flat notes, either side of the white notes.

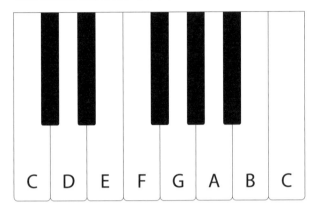

Play all these notes in order, black and white, to make a **chromatic scale** where all the notes are next door to one another. Notes next door to each other are a **semitone** apart.

Play your chromatic sc twice: once legato *and o staccat*

② Which pairs of notes do NOT have a black note in between? _____

_____

These notes are also a SEMITONE apart.
That means the notes are next door neighbours.

③ Which pairs of notes DO have a black note in between?_____

_____

These notes are a TONE apart:
two semitones equal one tone.

Know your tones and semitones

④ Play each of these after you have filled in the answer:

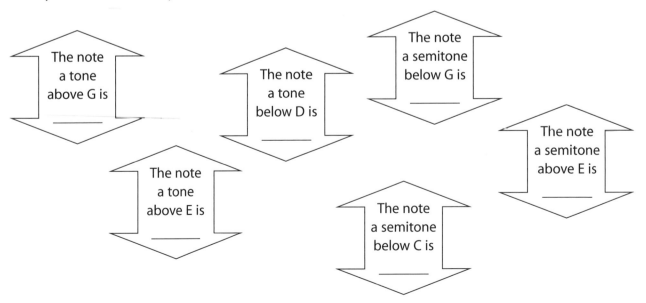

Major scales

Scales follow a set pattern of semitones and tones. Major scales follow this pattern:

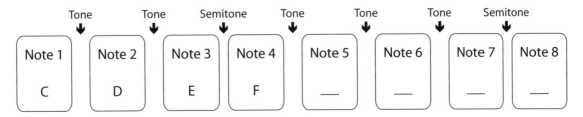

In the boxes above complete the note names for C major.

⑤ Using the pattern of tones and semitones given above, put a cross above the first five notes of a G major scale on this keyboard:

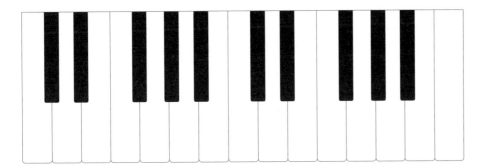

> *Play all the notes you mark: do they sound correct?*

⑥ Now put a circle on or above the first five notes of an F major scale: to keep the tones and semitones in the same order you'll need one black note here.

> *Can you play these notes in three contrasting ways?*

Getting to know scales

Play a scale in each of the following keys.

⑦ When you're happy with how they sound, fill in the notes that are played sharp or flat in each scale in the boxes below.

> *C major has no sharps or flats.*

C Major		
G Major		
D Major		
A Major		
B♭ Major		
F Major		

Do all the scales sound as if they have the same pattern of notes?
If not, check your tones and semitones again.

Key signatures

Pieces of music are usually based around the notes of a scale. This is known as the **key** of that piece, so some notes in the piece are always sharp or flat. To save writing a sharp or flat sign every time these notes are played, we write a **key signature** at the start of each line of music.

Choose a piece

Choose one of your pieces and answer the following:

Title of piece: _____

Key of piece: _____

If you transpose it up a tone it will be in: _____

The first right-hand note will be: _____

❏ Play the first two bars of the right hand up a tone.

To transpose a melody means to play it in a higher or lower key.

What's the key?

⑧ Play this melody. What key is it in? _____

   If you transpose it down a tone what key will it be in? _____

   What note will it start and finish on? _____

   What note(s) will you need to play sharp or
   flat in this new key to make it sound right? _____

❏ Circle any semitones in the piece.

❏ Now play it down a tone.

Remember to p musically: think about t dynamics, tempo and so

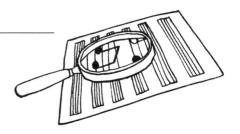

⑨ Play this melody. What key is it in? _____

   If you transpose it up a tone what key will it be in? _____

   What note will it start and finish on? _____

   What note(s) will you need to play sharp or
   flat in this new key to make it sound right? _____

❏ Now play it up a tone.

Playing in different keys

A melody for the right hand

Play this melody:

Transpose it into the following keys. Tick each when you have played it:
- ❏   D major
- ❏   F major
- ❏   G major

A melody for the left hand

The next exercise is for your left hand. Play it first, then transpose it into the keys listed below, ticking each when you've played it.

Remember to work out what sharps and flats you'll need to play.

- ❏   G major
- ❏   C major
- ❏   A major

A melody for both hands

The next melody is in the key of C major. Play first the left hand and then the right hand:

Moderato

Now play the same melody in the following keys with each hand separately, remembering if any notes need to be played sharp or flat. Tick each one when you have played it successfully.
- ❏   F major
- ❏   G major
- ❏   B♭ major

Now try each of these keys with both hands together.

Minor keys

Play these two phrases. The first phrase is in a major key, the second is minor.
Can you hear the difference? Try playing these two phrases in different ways.
Which one sounds happy and which one sounds sad?

Relative major and minor keys

All major keys have a **relative minor** which shares its key signature.
All minor keys have a **relative major** with the same key signature.

To find the relative minor of a major key you need to find the **sixth** note of
the major scale. If you are in C major the sixth note is A: so the relative
minor of C major is A minor.

⑩ What is the relative minor of the following major keys:

D major _____

B♭ major _____

To find the relative major of a minor key you need to find the **third** note of
the minor scale. If you are in A minor the third note is C: so the relative major
of A minor is C major.

⑪ What is the relative major of the following minor keys:

E minor _____

D minor _____

G minor _____

For more about min
keys, see Getting start
with theory page

Listen to some music on the radio and see if you can tell if it is in a major or minor key.

Which key?

To work out which key a piece of music is in you need to know how many
sharps or flats belong to each key signature (see *Getting to know scales* on
page 7). This could be either the relative major or minor. Looking at the first
and last notes and any accidentals should help you decide which key it is.
Look out for the 7th note: in minor keys it is often raised a semitone.

Finding minor pieces

How many of your pieces are in a minor key? See if you can find two and
answer these questions about them:

Title of piece: _____

Key of piece: _____ Relative major: _____

Title of piece: _____

Key of piece: _____ Relative major: _____

Naming notes of the scale

Tones and semitones are one way of measuring the distance between notes.
Another system **numbers** the notes rather like a staircase:

Use this staircase to fill in and work out note names.

❏　Next to each number fill in the letter names of a scale of C major.
❏　Here is the scale written on a stave. Below each note fill in its number:

Each note within a scale also has a **name**. Here are some of them:

The first note of any scale is called the **tonic**.
The fourth note of any scale is called the **subdominant**.
The fifth note of any scale is called the **dominant**.

⑫ What is the tonic note of G major? _____

What is the dominant note of C major? _____

What is the subdominant note of A minor? _____

Improvise a march using just the tonic, subdominant and dominant notes from your favourite scale.

⑬ Play the melody above. What key is it in? _____
　❏　Circle all the tonic notes you can find.
　❏　Put an x above all the dominant notes you can find.
　❏　Look at where the tonic and dominant notes are in the phrase.
　❏　Can you play the rest of this well-known melody?

Choose a different scale and improvise a fanfare using just the tonic, subdominant and dominant notes.

Choose a piece

Look at one of your pieces. What key is it in? _____

Name the tonic note: _____ dominant: _____ subdominant: _____

Play the first phrase: can you spot any of these notes in it? Describe where
they are and how they make this phrase sound:

_____

_____

Transposing tunes

As well as transposing up or down by tones or semitones, you may also need to play a piece in its dominant or subdominant key. To do this, first work out what key you are in, count up to the correct note to find the new tonic, then work out what sharps or flats you need to play.

Play each of the melodies below, answer the questions, then transpose each to its new key.

As you play each melo[dy] add some dynamics a[nd] articulation that you thi[nk] work we[ll]

Smoothly

⑭ What key is this in? _____   The subdominant note is: _____

Subdominant key: _____   New key signature: _____

Waltz

⑮ What key is this in? _____   The dominant note is: _____

Dominant key: _____   New key signature: _____

Try playing each melo[dy] at different octaves and w[ith] different han[ds]

Walking

⑯ What key is this in? _____   The subdominant note is: _____

Subdominant key: _____   New key signature: _____

Lullaby

⑰ What key is this in? _____   The dominant note is: _____

Dominant key: _____   New key signature: _____

Play the first four bars of your own pieces in their dominant and subdominant keys. Remember to try both left and right hands: each hand on its own first, then both together!

Chords and triads

When more than one note is played at the same time it is known as a **chord**.
A chord containing three notes is known as a **triad**. If we play the 1st, 3rd and
5th notes of a scale this is a **tonic triad**.

⑱ Fill in and play the notes of the tonic triads of the following keys:

Key	1st	3rd	5th
C Major	C		G
A minor	A		
G major		B	
D major	D		
B♭ Major			F

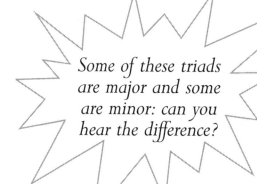

Some of these triads are major and some are minor: can you hear the difference?

Can you spot any tonic triads in your own pieces?

More triads

You can also build triads on other notes of the scale, such as the fourth and
fifth notes:

A triad built on the **fourth note** of a
scale is called the **subdominant triad**:

A triad built on the **fifth note** of a
scale is called the **dominant triad**:

*In minor keys, the
dominant triad contains the
raised 7th note of the scale.*

⑲ Here are the scales of F major and G major. Fill in and play the tonic,
subdominant and dominant triads above the correct notes in each scale:

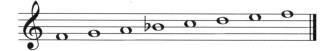

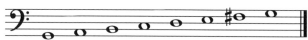

Choose a piece

Choose one of your pieces. Work out what key it is in, then with each
hand play:

- ❏ The tonic triad.
- ❏ The subdominant triad.
- ❏ The dominant triad.

*For more about triads
see Getting started with theory
page 19.*

Pick a box

Can you complete all of the following? Tick each when you've done it.
Remember, in minor keys the 7th note is raised.

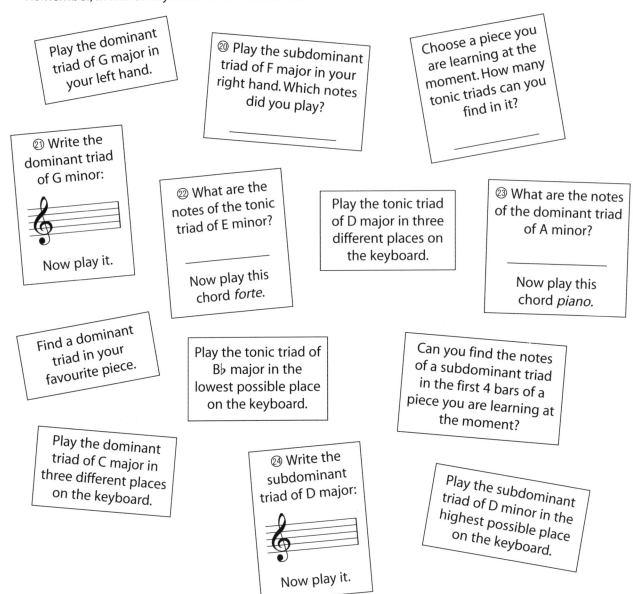

Play the dominant triad of G major in your left hand.

⑳ Play the subdominant triad of F major in your right hand. Which notes did you play?

_____

Choose a piece you are learning at the moment. How many tonic triads can you find in it?

_____

㉑ Write the dominant triad of G minor:

Now play it.

㉒ What are the notes of the tonic triad of E minor?

_____

Now play this chord *forte*.

Play the tonic triad of D major in three different places on the keyboard.

㉓ What are the notes of the dominant triad of A minor?

_____

Now play this chord *piano*.

Find a dominant triad in your favourite piece.

Play the tonic triad of B♭ major in the lowest possible place on the keyboard.

Can you find the notes of a subdominant triad in the first 4 bars of a piece you are learning at the moment?

Play the dominant triad of C major in three different places on the keyboard.

㉔ Write the subdominant triad of D major:

Now play it.

Play the subdominant triad of D minor in the highest possible place on the keyboard.

Numbering triads and chords

Triads and chords can also be numbered using Roman numerals:

1	2	3	4	5	6	7	(8)
I	II	III	IV	V	VI	VII	I

*A chord on the 8th r
is chord I ag*

㉕ What is the name of chord I? _____

Which number chord is the subdominant? _____

What is the name of chord V? _____

❑ Fill in the Roman numerals next to the numbers on your staircase on p.11.

Cadences

A **cadence** is a pattern of two chords which create a natural pause or ending in the music. Play this phrase:

Play it again and under the last two notes add a G followed by a C in your left hand. Any octave is fine – try different ones! You've just played a cadence. Does it change how the phrase sounds?

Perfect cadences

A **Perfect** cadence sounds final and uses these chords:

Dominant (chord V) → Tonic (chord I)

Here is a Perfect cadence in the key of C major. Try playing it. Can you hear how it sounds like the end of a piece or section?

Right hand uses one or more notes of the dominant chord (G B D)...

...followed by any note of the tonic chord (C E G).

Can you find a Perfect cadence in two of your pieces?

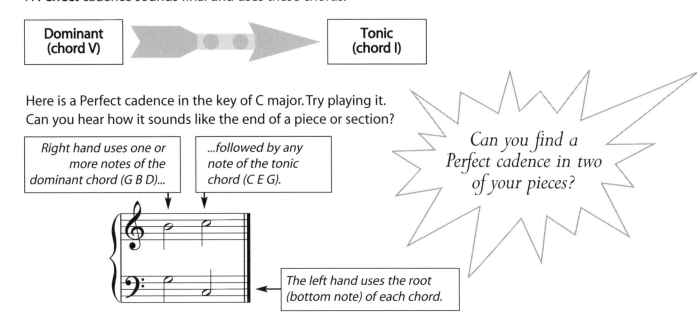

The left hand uses the root (bottom note) of each chord.

Complete this Perfect cadence in C major by filling in the right-hand notes. Play the left hand first, then try different notes from the chord in the right hand. Do some sound better than others? Fill in the notes you like best.

Try to avoid copying the left-hand notes in your right hand: it will make your chord sound thin.

Playing Perfect cadences

Work out and play a Perfect cadence in the following keys. Tick each one when you have played it successfully:

- ❑ G major; play it *legato* then *staccato*.
- ❑ F major; play it loudly then softly.
- ❑ A minor; play it slowly then quickly.

Can you make up a short tune and finish it with a Perfect cadence?

Plagal cadences

A **Plagal** cadence also sounds final, and uses these chords:

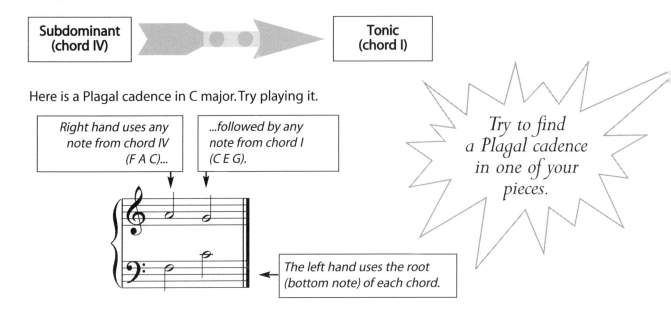

| Subdominant (chord IV) | ➡ | Tonic (chord I) |

Here is a Plagal cadence in C major. Try playing it.

Right hand uses any note from chord IV (F A C)...

...followed by any note from chord I (C E G).

Try to find a Plagal cadence in one of your pieces.

The left hand uses the root (bottom note) of each chord.

Choose suitable right-hand notes to complete these Plagal cadences. Play them first, then fill in the notes you like best:

Can you make up a sh tune and finish it wit Plagal caden

Plagal or Perfect?

㉖ These cadences are either Plagal or Perfect. Play them and try to work out which is which by how they sound. Then work out the keys and check the notes to see if you were right!

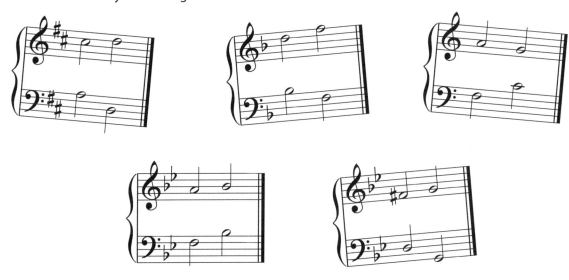

Imperfect cadences

The **Imperfect cadence** sounds unfinished, as if the music will continue. It uses the tonic followed by the dominant chord:

Play this cadence. Then go back to page 15 and play the Perfect cadence again. Can you hear the difference between the two?

Work out and play a Perfect and then an Imperfect cadence in each of the following keys. Tick each one when you have done it:

❏ G major

❏ F major

❏ A minor

Interrupted cadences

Think of this as the 'surprise' cadence. It uses chord V then chord VI. In a major key this takes us unexpectedly to a minor key (the relative minor). In a minor key this takes us unexpectedly to a major key (the relative major). Play this interrupted cadence in C major:

Can you make up a short tune and finish it with an Imperfect or Interrupted cadence?

Chord connections

㉗ Play each of these cadences, then draw a line to connect each cadence to its correct name:

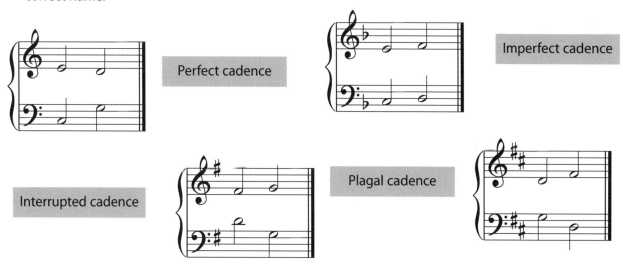

Perfect cadence

Imperfect cadence

Interrupted cadence

Plagal cadence

Playing three-part cadences

So far we have played two-part cadences with one note in the left hand and one note in the right hand. With a three-part cadence you can still play the root of the chord in the left hand and any two notes from the triad in the right hand.

Try playing this three-part Perfect cadence in C major:

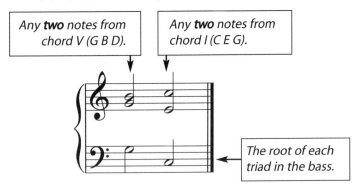

Any **two** notes from chord V (G B D).

Any **two** notes from chord I (C E G).

The root of each triad in the bass.

You will find it sounds more musical if the notes move in contrary motion.

Now play the same cadence but with different pairs of notes for the right hand. Listen carefully: which notes sound best?

For each of the following keys, play and then tick the boxes below:
  1 The scale of the key with your right hand.
  2 The scale of the key with your left hand.
  3 The three-part cadence listed.
  4 The same cadence with a different combination of right-hand notes.

	1	2		3	4
C Major	❏	❏	Plagal cadence	❏	❏
G Major	❏	❏	Imperfect cadence	❏	❏
A Minor	❏	❏	Perfect cadence	❏	❏
F Major	❏	❏	Interrupted cadence	❏	❏
D Minor	❏	❏	Imperfect cadence	❏	❏

Can you make up a s tune and finish it wi three-part Perfect cader

Spot the cadence

㉘ Can you name the key and the cadence each time? Make sure you play them first.

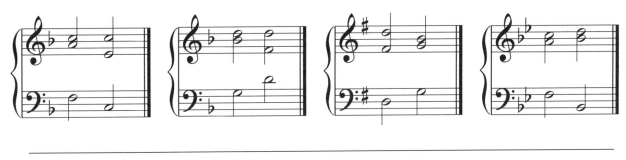

Three-part cadence boxes

Choose a box and see if you can complete the task!

Play a Plagal cadence in F major. Write it below:

Find a Perfect cadence in one of your pieces. Play the cadence and write the title of the piece:

_____

㉙ Name a cadence which makes a piece sound as though it will continue:

_____

Play one in G major.

㉚ What key is this in and what is the cadence?

_____

Play a Perfect cadence in the key of your favourite piece.

Play and then write an Imperfect cadence in D major:

Play and then complete a Plagal cadence above these notes:

Play a Plagal cadence in the key of your favourite piece.

Pick a piece you are learning at the moment. How many Perfect cadences can you find in it?

_____

㉛ Play this cadence then fill in its name and key:

Play a cadence in A minor which sounds finished. Now write it down:

Play and then complete a Perfect cadence below these notes:

Can you find a Plagal cadence in any of your pieces? Play the cadence and write the title here:

_____

Play this phrase and end it with a Perfect cadence:

Tackling transposition

Looking for clues

As you begin to transpose longer phrases and start to transpose with both hands together, you need to look out for clues in the music to help you.

Here is a melody in C major:

Can you see these clues?
- ❏ It starts and ends on the tonic note.
- ❏ The 1st bar uses the notes of the tonic chord.
- ❏ The 2nd bar is centred around the dominant note.
- ❏ The 3rd bar contains two descending leaps of a 3rd.

Play it through several times until you know it well. Can you play it from memory? Remembering all your clues:

❏ Transpose it up a tone.

㉜ The new key will be: _____ Key signature: _____

❏ Transpose it to the dominant.

㉝ The new key will be: _____ Key signature: _____

This melody contains more leaps. Can you spot the clues listed below?

- ❏ It is in G major and starts and ends on the tonic note.
- ❏ The leaps in the first 3 bars are all between the notes of the tonic chord.
- ❏ The whole melody covers an octave.

Make sure you play musically: try out dynamics and articulation. When you're happy with them, add them to the music.

Play it through several times until you know it well; first with your right hand and then an octave lower in your left hand. Can you play it from memory?

㉞ What is the subdominant of this key? _____

㉟ What is the dominant? _____

❏ Transpose the melody into each of these keys with each hand in turn.

Finding your own clues

Play this melody in your left hand:

Can you add a Perfect cadence at the end of this phrase?

This time, make your own list of its features. Mention things like the key, any patterns you can see and the way the melody moves:

_____

_____

_____

Play it through once more then transpose it to the following keys. Tick each one after you have done it correctly:

- ❑ Transpose it up a tone.
- ❑ Transpose it into F major.
- ❑ Transpose it down a tone.

Minor melody clues

This next melody is in the key of A minor – watch out for the accidentals!

Can you add a cadence at the end of this phrase? Which cadence works best?

Play it through several times to get to know it, then list its features:

_____

_____

_____

❑ Transpose it down a tone to the key of G minor.
What will its key signature and any accidentals be?

_____

❑ Play the melody in the dominant key and then the subdominant key with each hand in turn. Did you play the correct accidentals?

Remember your list of features as you play in the new keys.

Choose a piece

Write a list of clues for the first 4 bars of the melody line of one of your pieces. Now choose a key to transpose it to and see if you can play it.

_____

_____

Transposing with both hands

To transpose a piece with both hands together you need to remember your clues. You'll also need to think about the chords being used. Play this:

㊱ Which cadence do these two bars end with? _____

❏ If you transposed this to the dominant, what would the notes of the left hand be? _____ Play it in this key.

❏ Work out the notes to transpose it to the subdominant key, then play it.

In this piece, you should notice that in the right hand:
❏   Bars 1 and 2 use notes of the tonic chord.
❏   Bar 3 is a descending scale down to the tonic note.
❏   Bar 4 repeats the tonic note.
And in the left hand:
❏   Bars 1, 2 and 4 are the same note.
❏   Bar 3 is a semitone lower.

❏ Transpose it to the subdominant key and play it *legato*.
❏ Transpose it to the dominant key and play it *forte*.

Add a dynamic to these two phrases: what do you think sounds best? Do the crotchets sound better played legato or staccato?

Here is another example. Look through it carefully before playing it:

This time make your own list of clues:

_____

❏ Transpose it to the subdominant key, then the dominant key.

Here are some more pieces. Look through each for clues and assess which chords are being used. Play them through, then transpose each as directed.

㊲ Transpose up a tone. The new key is _____

Can you complete the rest of any of these well-known melodies?

㊳ Transpose down a tone. The new key is _____

㊴ Transpose up a tone. The new key is _____

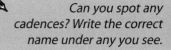

Can you spot any cadences? Write the correct name under any you see.

㊵ Transpose to the subdominant. The new key is _____

㊶ Transpose up a tone. The new key is _____

Exploring further

❏ Can you complete these 4-bar tunes and add a cadence at the end of each?
Experiment to see which cadence sounds best and how they change the
character of the melody.

*For more about wr.
your own tunes see* Get
started with composi*

❏ Play the first phrase of several pieces you know well. Then transpose each
phrase to the dominant and subdominant keys. Make a list of the pieces
here and fill in the key of the subdominant and dominant as you play them.

Title of piece	subdominant key	dominant key

❏ Play a tune you know well by ear; then add a cadence to it. Experiment with
different cadences until you decide which sounds best.

❏ Choose a key and improvise a melody of two phrases. Let the first end with a
Perfect cadence and the second with a Plagal cadence. You will have to work
out which notes to include in the melody to fit each cadence!

❏ Choose a key and improvise a melody of two phrases. This time include an
Imperfect and Perfect cadence at the end of each phrase. Make sure the
notes you use will fit each cadence!

❏ Improvise a melody of four short phrases and include all four cadences in it.
Write your melody out below: